LIFE
Lessons

WITH MAX LUCADO

BOOKS OF
1 & 2 PETER

BETWEEN THE ROCK
AND A HARD PLACE

MAX LUCADO

Prepared by

THE LIVINGSTONE CORPORATION

THOMAS NELSON
Since 1798

NASHVILLE   DALLAS   MEXICO CITY   RIO DE JANEIRO   BEIJING

Life Lessons with Max Lucado—Books of 1 & 2 Peter

Copyright © by Thomas Nelson, 2007

Published in Nashville, Tennessee. Thomas Nelson is a trademark of Thomas Nelson, Inc.

Thomas Nelson, Inc. titles may be purchased in bulk for educational, business, fundraising, or sales promotional use. For information, please email SpecialMarkets@ThomasNelson.com.

Produced with the assistance of the Livingstone Corporation (www.livingstonecorp.com). Project staff include Jake Barton, Joel Bartlett, Andy Culbertson, Mary Horner Collins, and Will Reaves.

Editor: Neil Wilson

Scripture quotations marked "NCV™" are taken from the New Century Version®. Copyright © 2005 by Thomas Nelson, Inc. Used by permission. All rights reserved.

Scripture quotations marked "NKJV™" are taken from the New King James Version®. Copyright © 1982 by Thomas Nelson, Inc. Used by permission. All rights reserved.

Scripture quotations marked (NIV) are taken from the Holy Bible, New International Version. Copyright © 1973, 1978, 1984 by International Bible Society. All rights reserved. Use by permission of Zondervan Publishing House.

Material for the "Inspiration" sections taken from the following books:

A Love Worth Giving. Copyright © 2002 by Max Lucado. W Publishing Group, a Division of Thomas Nelson, Inc., Nashville, Tennessee.

The Applause of Heaven. Copyright © 1990, 1996, 1999 by Max Lucado. W Publishing Group, a Division of Thomas Nelson, Inc., Nashville, Tennessee.

He Still Moves Stones. Copyright © 1993 by Max Lucado. W Publishing Group, a Division of Thomas Nelson, Inc., Nashville, Tennessee.

In the Eye of the Storm. Copyright © 1991 by Max Lucado. W Publishing Group, a Division of Thomas Nelson, Inc., Nashville, Tennessee.

Just Like Jesus. Copyright © 2003 by Max Lucado. W Publishing Group, a Division of Thomas Nelson, Inc., Nashville, Tennessee.

Next Door Savior. Copyright © 2003 by Max Lucado. W Publishing Group, a Division of Thomas Nelson, Inc., Nashville, Tennessee.

Shaped by God (previously published as *On the Anvil*). Copyright © 2001 by Max Lucado. Tyndale House Publishers, Wheaton, Illinois.

Six Hours One Friday. Copyright © 2004 by Max Lucado. W Publishing Group, a Division of Thomas Nelson, Inc., Nashville, Tennessee.

Traveling Light. Copyright © 2001 by Max Lucado. W Publishing Group, a Division of Thomas Nelson, Inc., Nashville, Tennessee.

Cover Art and Interior Design by Kirk Luttrell of the Livingstone Corporation

Interior Composition by Rachel Hawkins of the Livingstone Corporation

ISBN-10: 1-4185-0957-4

ISBN-13: 978-1-4185-0957-6

Printed in the United States of America.

07 08 09 10 11 12 13 14 15 RRD 9 8 7 6 5 4 3 2 1

LIFE Lessons

WITH MAX LUCADO

CONTENTS

How to Study the Bible		iv
Introduction to the Book of 1 Peter		vii
Lesson 1	A Living Hope	1
Lesson 2	New Life in Christ	11
Lesson 3	Jesus Christ, the Cornerstone	21
Lesson 4	Following Jesus' Example	31
Lesson 5	Holy Living	41
Lesson 6	Loving People	51
Lesson 7	Joyful Service	61
Lesson 8	Trusting God Through Trials	71
Lesson 9	Humility	81
	Introduction to the Book of 2 Peter	90
Lesson 10	Self-Discipline	91
Lesson 11	False Teachers	101
Lesson 12	God Is in Control	111

HOW TO
STUDY THE BIBLE

This is a peculiar book you are holding. Words crafted in another language. Deeds done in a distant era. Events recorded in a far-off land. Counsel offered to a foreign people. This is a peculiar book.

It's surprising that anyone reads it. It's too old. Some of its writings date back five thousand years. It's too bizarre. The book speaks of incredible floods, fires, earthquakes, and people with supernatural abilities. It's too radical. The Bible calls for undying devotion to a carpenter who called himself God's Son.

Logic says this book shouldn't survive. Too old, too bizarre, too radical.

The Bible has been banned, burned, scoffed, and ridiculed. Scholars have mocked it as foolish. Kings have branded it as illegal. A thousand times over, the grave has been dug and the dirge has begun, but somehow the Bible never stays in the grave. Not only has it survived; it has thrived. It is the single most popular book in all of history. It has been the best-selling book in the world for years!

There is no way on earth to explain it. Which perhaps is the only explanation. The answer? The Bible's durability is not found on earth; it is found in heaven. For the millions who have tested its claims and claimed its promises, there is but one answer: the Bible is God's book and God's voice.

As you read it, you would be wise to give some thought to two questions. What is the purpose of the Bible? and How do I study the Bible? Time spent reflecting on these two issues will greatly enhance your Bible study.

What is the purpose of the Bible?

Let the Bible itself answer that question.

Since you were a child you have known the Holy Scriptures which are able to make you wise. And that wisdom leads to salvation through faith in Christ Jesus. (2 Tim. 3:15 NCV)

The purpose of the Bible? Salvation. God's highest passion is to get his children home. His book, the Bible, describes his plan of salvation. The purpose of the Bible is to proclaim God's plan and passion to save his children.

That is the reason this book has endured through the centuries. It dares to tackle the toughest questions about life: Where do I go after I die? Is there a God? What do I do with my fears? The Bible offers answers to these crucial questions. It is the treasure map that leads us to God's highest treasure, eternal life.

But how do we use the Bible? Countless copies of Scripture sit unread on bookshelves and nightstands simply because people don't know how to read it. What can we do to make the Bible real in our lives?

The clearest answer is found in the words of Jesus. He promised:

Ask, and God will give to you. Search, and you will find. Knock, and the door will open for you. (Matt. 7:7 NCV)

The first step in understanding the Bible is asking God to help us. We should read prayerfully. If anyone understands God's Word, it is because of God and not the reader.

But the Helper will teach you everything and will cause you to remember all that I told you. The Helper is the Holy Spirit whom the Father will send in my name. (John 14:26 NCV)

Before reading the Bible, pray. Invite God to speak to you. Don't go to Scripture looking for your idea; go searching for his.

Not only should we read the Bible prayerfully; we should read it carefully. *Search and you will find* is the pledge. The Bible is not a newspaper to be skimmed but rather a mine to be quarried.

Search for it like silver, and hunt for it like hidden treasure. Then you will understand respect for the LORD, and you will find that you know God. (Prov. 2:4–5 NCV)

Any worthy find requires effort. The Bible is no exception. To understand the Bible you don't have to be brilliant, but you must be willing to roll up your sleeves and search.

Be a worker who is not ashamed and who uses the true teaching in the right way. (2 Tim. 2:15 NCV)

Here's a practical point. Study the Bible a bit at a time. Hunger is not satisfied by eating twenty-one meals in one sitting once a week. The body needs a steady diet to remain strong. So does the soul. When God sent food to his people in the wilderness, he didn't provide loaves already made. Instead, he sent them manna in the shape of *"thin flakes like frost . . . on the desert ground"* (Ex. 16:14 NCV).

God gave manna in limited portions. God sends spiritual food the same way. He opens the heavens with just enough nutrients for today's hunger. He provides *"a command here, a command there. A rule here, a rule there. A little lesson here, a little lesson there"* (Isa. 28:10 NCV).

Don't be discouraged if your reading reaps a small harvest. Some days a lesser portion is all that is needed. What is important is to search every day for that day's message. A steady diet of God's Word over a lifetime builds a healthy soul and mind.

A little girl returned from her first day at school. Her mom asked, "Did you learn anything?"

"Apparently not enough," the girl responded, "I have to go back tomorrow and the next day and the next . . ."

Such is the case with learning. And such is the case with Bible study. Understanding comes little by little over a lifetime.

There is a third step in understanding the Bible. After the asking and seeking comes the knocking. After you ask and search, then knock.

Knock, and the door will open for you. (Matt. 7:7 NCV)

To knock is to stand at God's door. To make yourself available. To climb the steps, cross the porch, stand at the doorway, and volunteer. Knocking goes beyond the realm of thinking and into the realm of acting.

To knock is to ask, What can I do? How can I obey? Where can I go?

It's one thing to know what to do. It's another to do it. But for those who do it, those who choose to obey, a special reward awaits them.

The truly happy are those who carefully study God's perfect law that makes people free, and they continue to study it. They do not forget what they heard, but they obey what God's teaching says. Those who do this will be made happy. (James 1:25 NCV)

What a promise. Happiness comes to those who do what they read! It's the same with medicine. If you only read the label but ignore the pills, it won't help. It's the same with food. If you only read the recipe but never cook, you won't be fed. And it's the same with the Bible. If you only read the words but never obey, you'll never know the joy God has promised.

Ask. Search. Knock. Simple, isn't it? Why don't you give it a try? If you do, you'll see why you are holding the most remarkable book in history.

INTRODUCTION TO THE BOOK OF 1 PETER

It's not easy being the only one in your family who goes to church. It's bad enough that they don't go. It's worse that they make fun of you for going.

If you would pad your expense account, so could the other salesmen. But if you don't, they can't. "Come on," they urge you. "Just hedge a little." You refuse. The next day someone has spilled paint on your car.

Persecution. Not by firing squad. Not by death threats. Not by the government. But it's persecution nonetheless. A more subtle persecution. Persecution from friends, family, and peers. They won't take your life . . . but they will take your peace . . . and they'd like to take your faith, if you'll let them.

How do you respond? Begin with Peter's survival manual. He understood persecution. Beaten and jailed. Threatened and punished. He knew the sting of the false word and the angry whip. No doubt he'd seen some Christians stand and others fall. He'd seen enough to know what it takes to stay strong in tough times.

His counsel may surprise you.

His counsel may sustain you. It may be just what you need so that "the purity of your faith will bring you praise and glory and honor when Jesus Christ is shown to you" (1:7 NCV).

A LIVING HOPE

MAX
LUCADO

REFLECTION

It may just be a coincidence that "hope" and "cope" rhyme, but it's a happy coincidence. If we can't see beyond our immediate circumstances in life, the outlook quickly turns to a shade of despair. Consider a time, recently or in the past, when you felt hopeless about a situation in your life. How did you cope? What would have helped you during that time?

SITUATION

Whether he was fishing or, later, following Jesus as his disciple, Peter was passionate. Filled with the Holy Spirit at Pentecost, Peter boldly preached in Jerusalem and became a founding apostle of the early church. By the time Peter wrote this letter, the gospel had reached Rome and far beyond. Believers had been scattered due to opposition and violent persecution. Peter was probably aware that his own time was short. These letters have become a beacon of hope to any believer down through the centuries going through hard times. For such times as these, Peter had some wisdom to share.

OBSERVATION

Read 1 Peter 1:1—12 from the NCV or the NKJV.

NCV

¹From Peter, an apostle of Jesus Christ.

To God's chosen people who are away from their homes and are scattered all around the countries of Pontus, Galatia, Cappadocia, Asia, and Bithynia. ²God planned long ago to choose you by making you his holy people, which is the Spirit's work. God wanted you to obey him and to be made clean by the blood of the death of Jesus Christ.

Grace and peace be yours more and more.

3Praise be to the God and Father of our Lord Jesus Christ. In God's great mercy he has caused us to be born again into a living hope, because Jesus Christ rose from the dead. 4Now we hope for the blessings God has for his children. These blessings, which cannot be destroyed or be spoiled or lose their beauty, are kept in heaven for you. 5God's power protects you through your faith until salvation is shown to you at the end of time.

6This makes you very happy, even though now for a short time different kinds of troubles may make you sad. 7These troubles come to prove that your faith is pure. This purity of faith is worth more than gold, which can be proved to be pure by fire but will ruin. But the purity of your faith will bring you praise and glory and honor when Jesus Christ is shown to you. 8You have not seen Christ, but still you love him. You cannot see him now, but you believe in him. So you are filled with a joy that cannot be explained, a joy full of glory. 9And you are receiving the goal of your faith—the salvation of your souls.

10The prophets searched carefully and tried to learn about this salvation. They prophesied about the grace that was coming to you. 11The Spirit of Christ was in the prophets, telling in advance about the sufferings of Christ and about the glory that would follow those sufferings. The prophets tried to learn about what the Spirit was showing them, when those things would happen, and what the world would be like at that time. 12It was shown them that their service was not for themselves but for you, when they told about the truths you have now heard. Those who preached the Good News to you told you those things with the help of the Holy Spirit who was sent from heaven—things into which angels desire to look.

NKJV

Peter, an apostle of Jesus Christ,

1To the pilgrims of the Dispersion in Pontus, Galatia, Cappadocia, Asia, and Bithynia, 2elect according to the foreknowledge of God the Father, in sanctification of the Spirit, for obedience and sprinkling of the blood of Jesus Christ:

Grace to you and peace be multiplied.

3Blessed be the God and Father of our Lord Jesus Christ, who according to His abundant mercy has begotten us again to a living hope through the resurrection of Jesus Christ from the dead, 4to an inheritance incorruptible and undefiled and that does not fade away, reserved in heaven for you, 5who are kept by the power of God through faith for salvation ready to be revealed in the last time.

6In this you greatly rejoice, though now for a little while, if need be, you have been grieved by various trials, 7that the genuineness of your faith, being much more precious than gold that perishes, though it is tested by fire, may be found to praise, honor, and glory at the revelation of Jesus Christ, 8whom having not seen you love. Though now you do not see Him, yet believing, you rejoice with joy inexpressible and full of glory, 9receiving the end of your faith—the salvation of your souls.

[10]*Of this salvation the prophets have inquired and searched carefully, who prophesied of the grace that would come to you,* [11]*searching what, or what manner of time, the Spirit of Christ who was in them was indicating when He testified beforehand the sufferings of Christ and the glories that would follow.* [12]*To them it was revealed that, not to themselves, but to us they were ministering the things which now have been reported to you through those who have preached the gospel to you by the Holy Spirit sent from heaven—things which angels desire to look into.*

EXPLORATION

1. What does it mean to our everyday lives that God plans to make us holy? How does he accomplish this?

2. In what ways do you consider your salvation "a blessing"?

3. How would you describe a pure faith? How does Peter describe it in these verses?

4. How can our hope in Jesus help us endure trials?

5. In what way have the trials in your life strengthened your faith?

INSPIRATION

There is something about a living testimony that gives us courage. Once we see someone else emerging from life's dark tunnels we realize that we, too, can overcome.

Could this be why Jesus is called our pioneer? Is this one of the reasons that he consented to enter the horrid chambers of death? It must be. His words, though persuasive, were not enough. His promises, though true, didn't quite allay the fear of the people. His actions, even the act of calling Lazarus from the tomb, didn't convince the crowds that death was nothing to fear. No. In the eyes of humanity, death was still the black veil that separated them from joy. There was no victory over this hooded foe. Its putrid odor invaded the nostrils of every human, convincing them that life was only meant to end abruptly and senselessly.

It was left to the Son of God to disclose the true nature of this force. It was on the cross that the showdown occurred. Christ called for Satan's cards. Weary of seeing humanity fooled by a coverup, he entered the tunnel of death to prove that there was indeed an exit. And, as the world darkened, creation held her breath.

Satan threw his best punch, but it wasn't enough. Even the darkness of hell's tunnel was no match for God's Son. Even the chambers of Hades couldn't stop this Raider. Legions of screaming demons held nothing over the Lion of Judah.

Christ emerged from death's tunnel, lifted a triumphant fist toward the sky, and freed all from the fear of death. "Death has been swallowed up in victory!" (From *Shaped by God* by Max Lucado)

REACTION

6. What are some ways that Christ's victory over death encourages you?

7. How would your life be different if Christ had not conquered death?

8. In what way does your hope for the future change the way you live each day?

9. What does it mean to rejoice in your salvation?

10. How does this passage affect your attitude toward the trials in your life?

11. What words of hope from this passage do you want to remember the next time you face trials?

LIFE LESSONS

Peter not only describes a hopeful life in this passage; he demonstrates one. He speaks to his readers as if they are already doing what they need to do in their circumstances, trusting fully in God. His hope for them is unconditional. We will always face difficulties, but we can face them assured that the Lord is with us, and he will see to it that his purposes are accomplished in us. That is hopeful living!

DEVOTION

Father, help us see the joy that is before us. You have given us such a great treasure—the promise of salvation. Forgive us, Father, for losing sight of our glorious future. Renew our vision and help us strain toward the goal of our faith—the salvation of our souls. And when we face trials, remind us that you have won the ultimate victory.

For more Bible passages on hope, see Psalms 42:5; 130:7; Proverbs 23:17–18; Jeremiah 29:11; Romans 8:24–25; 15:4, 13; 1 Corinthians 15:19–32; Colossians 1:27; 1 Thessalonians 1:3; Titus 1:2; 2:11–13; Hebrews 10:23.

To complete the books of 1 & 2 Peter during this twelve-part study, read 1 Peter 1:1–12.

JOURNALING

What are the blessings God has given me?

NEW LIFE IN CHRIST

MAX LUCADO

REFLECTION

Think of your lifestyle before you became a Christian. List some of the components of that life that you still treasure. Identify some of the issues that drove you to consider Jesus seriously. How is your life different now? How is it the same?

SITUATION

Peter wanted his brothers and sisters in the faith to have a genuine rather than a false hope. He pointed out to them some of the lies that might lead even a believer to cling to this life in a false sense of security and meaning. Temporal and material things cannot sustain hope. Genuine hope rests in God and his unchanging eternal plans.

OBSERVATION

Read 1 Peter 1:13—25 from the NCV or the NKJV.

NCV

13So prepare your minds for service and have self-control. All your hope should be for the gift of grace that will be yours when Jesus Christ is shown to you. 14Now that you are obedient children of God do not live as you did in the past. You did not understand, so you did the evil things you wanted. 15But be holy in all you do, just as God, the One who called you, is holy. 16It is written in the Scriptures: "You must be holy, because I am holy."

17You pray to God and call him Father, and he judges each person's work equally. So while you are here on earth, you should live with respect for God. 18You know that in the past you were living in a worthless way, a way passed down from the people who lived before you. But you were saved from that useless life. You were bought, not with something that ruins like gold or silver, 19but with the precious blood of Christ, who was like a pure and perfect lamb. 20Christ was chosen before the world was made, but he was shown to the world in these last times for your sake.

21Through Christ you believe in God, who raised Christ from the dead and gave him glory. So your faith and your hope are in God.

22Now that you have made your souls pure by obeying the truth, you can have true love for your Christian brothers and sisters. So love each other deeply with all your heart.

23You have been born again, and this new life did not come from something that dies, but from something that cannot die. You were born again through God's living message that continues forever. 24The Scripture says,

> "All people are like the grass,
>
> and all their glory is like the flowers of the field.
>
> The grass dies and the flowers fall,
>
> 25but the word of the Lord will live forever."

And this is the word that was preached to you.

NKJV

13Therefore gird up the loins of your mind, be sober, and rest your hope fully upon the grace that is to be brought to you at the revelation of Jesus Christ; 14as obedient children, not conforming yourselves to the former lusts, as in your ignorance; 15but as He who called you is holy, you also be holy in all your conduct, 16because it is written, "Be holy, for I am holy."

17And if you call on the Father, who without partiality judges according to each one's work, conduct yourselves throughout the time of your stay here in fear; 18knowing that you were not redeemed with corruptible things, like silver or gold, from your aimless conduct received by tradition from your fathers, 19but with the precious blood of Christ, as of a lamb without blemish and without spot. 20He indeed was foreordained before the foundation of the world, but was manifest in these last times for you 21who through Him believe in God, who raised Him from the dead and gave Him glory, so that your faith and hope are in God.

22Since you have purified your souls in obeying the truth through the Spirit in sincere love of the brethren, love one another fervently with a pure heart, 23having been born again, not of corruptible seed but incorruptible, through the word of God which lives and abides forever, 24because

> "All flesh is as grass,
>
> And all the glory of man as the flower of the grass.
>
> The grass withers,
>
> And its flower falls away,
>
> 25But the word of the LORD endures forever."

Now this is the word which by the gospel was preached to you.

EXPLORATION

1. How do our lives change after conversion?

2. What does it mean to be holy?

3. What motivates us to live righteously?

4. Why is it important to understand the price Jesus paid for our salvation?

5. This passage says that being pure enables us to demonstrate true love to others. What is the relationship between being pure and showing love?

INSPIRATION

Most of us had a hard time learning to tie our shoes. Squirting toothpaste on a brush was tough enough, but tightening shoes by wrapping strings together? Nothing easy about that. Besides, who needs them? Wear loafers. Go barefoot. Who came up with the idea of shoes anyhow?

And knees don't help. Always in your face. Leaning around them, pushing them away—a person can't concentrate.

And, oh, the advice! Everyone had a different approach. "Make a tree with the loop, and let the squirrel run around it into the hole." "Shape a rabbit ear, and then wrap it with a ribbon." Dad said, "Go fast." Your uncle said to take your time. Can't anyone agree? Only on one thing. You need to know how.

Learning to tie your shoes is a rite of passage. Right in there with first grade and first bike is first shoe tying. But, oh, how dreadful is the process.

Just when you think you've made the loops and circled the tree . . . you get the rabbit ears in either hand and give them a triumphant yank and, voila!—a knot. Unbeknownst to you, you've just been inducted into reality.

My friend Roy used to sit on a park bench for a few minutes each morning. He liked to watch the kids gather and play at the bus stop. One day he noticed a little fellow, maybe five or six years of age, struggling to board the bus. While others were climbing on, he was leaning down, frantically trying to disentangle a knotted shoestring. He grew more anxious by the moment, frantic eyes darting back and forth between the shoe and the ride.

All of a sudden it was too late. The door closed.

The boy fell back on his haunches and sighed. That's when he saw Roy. With tear-filled eyes he looked at the man on the bench and asked, "Do you untie knots?"

Jesus loves that request.

Life gets tangled. People mess up. You never outgrow the urge to look up and say, "Help!"

Jesus had a way of appearing at such moments. Peter's empty boat. Nicodemus' empty heart. Matthew has a friend issue. A woman has a health issue. Look who shows up.

Jesus, our next door Savior.

"Do you untie knots?"

"Yes." (From *Next Door Savior* by Max Lucado)

REACTION

6. How does this illustration of shoe tying and tangled laces help you relate to Peter's words about being obedient, holy, and pure?

7. How would you explain what it means to be "redeemed" to a friend with no religious background?

8. Who helped you realize your need for a spiritual transformation that only God could accomplish?

9. In what ways do we sometimes trivialize Christ's sacrifice?

10. Why is it difficult to change our ways after we are born again?

11. What old habits have you needed God's help to give up?

LIFE LESSONS

We have been charged to "gird up the loins of our minds" and make sure our spiritual shoelaces have been tied. The Christian life involves action, intention, and obedience. We must learn not to rely on those things that wither and fade, but instead to rely on what God tells us in his Word.

The way we live each day demonstrates how highly we value what Jesus has done for us.

DEVOTION

Father, we thank you for the gift of grace that is ours through Jesus Christ. We claim your salvation and ask you to help us respond with humility and obedience. Father, you have commanded us to be holy, just as you are holy. But we can do nothing without you. So we ask you to work through us, by your Spirit, and transform us into your likeness.

For more Bible passages on spiritual rebirth, see John 3:3–8; 2 Corinthians 5:17; Galatians 6:15; Ephesians 2:4–10; Titus 3:3–7; 1 Peter 1:3; 1 John 3:9.

To complete the books of 1 & 2 Peter during this twelve-part study, read 1 Peter 1:13–25.

LIFE LESSONS WITH MAX LUCADO

JOURNALING

What evidence of new life in Christ can I see in myself?

JESUS CHRIST, THE CORNERSTONE

MAX LUCADO

REFLECTION

Bring up Jesus Christ in a conversation and you're likely to get some strong reactions. What are some typical responses you've heard about who Jesus is? Why do you think people either hate and ignore him, or love him?

SITUATION

Jesus said, "On this rock I will build my church" (Matt. 16:18 NKJV). Stone has many qualities, not all of them desirable in a person. Yet Peter overcame most of the natural drawbacks in rock-living by using the term "living stone" when he referred to Jesus and to us. This oxymoron captures in a beautiful way the combination of engagement with the world and allegiance to Christ that ought to characterize the life of a believer.

OBSERVATION

Read 1 Peter 2:1—10 from the NCV or the NKJV.

NCV

¹So then, rid yourselves of all evil, all lying, hypocrisy, jealousy, and evil speech. ²As newborn babies want milk, you should want the pure and simple teaching. By it you can grow up and be saved, ³because you have already examined and seen how good the Lord is.

⁴Come to the Lord Jesus, the "stone" that lives. The people of the world did not want this stone, but he was the stone God chose, and he was precious. ⁵You also are like living stones, so let yourselves be used to build a spiritual temple—to be holy priests who offer spiritual sacrifices to God. He will accept those sacrifices through Jesus Christ. ⁶The Scripture says:

"I will put a stone in the ground in Jerusalem.

Everything will be built on this important and precious rock.

Anyone who trusts in him

will never be disappointed."

⁷*This stone is worth much to you who believe. But to the people who do not believe,*

> *"the stone that the builders rejected*
>
> *has become the cornerstone."*

⁸*Also, he is*

> *"a stone that causes people to stumble,*
>
> *a rock that makes them fall."*

They stumble because they do not obey what God says, which is what God planned to happen to them.

⁹*But you are a chosen people, royal priests, a holy nation, a people for God's own possession. You were chosen to tell about the wonderful acts of God, who called you out of darkness into his wonderful light.* ¹⁰*At one time you were not a people, but now you are God's people. In the past you had never received mercy, but now you have received God's mercy.*

NKJV

¹*Therefore, laying aside all malice, all deceit, hypocrisy, envy, and all evil speaking,* ²*as newborn babes, desire the pure milk of the word, that you may grow thereby,* ³*if indeed you have tasted that the Lord is gracious.*

⁴*Coming to Him as to a living stone, rejected indeed by men, but chosen by God and precious,* ⁵*you also, as living stones, are being built up a spiritual house, a holy priesthood, to offer up spiritual sacrifices acceptable to God through Jesus Christ.* ⁶*Therefore it is also contained in the Scripture,*

> *"Behold, I lay in Zion*
>
> *A chief cornerstone, elect, precious,*
>
> *And he who believes on Him will*
>
> *by no means be put to shame."*

⁷*Therefore, to you who believe, He is precious; but to those who are disobedient,*

> *"The stone which the builders rejected*
>
> *Has become the chief cornerstone,"*

⁸*and*

> *"A stone of stumbling*
>
> *And a rock of offense."*

They stumble, being disobedient to the word, to which they also were appointed.

⁹*But you are a chosen generation, a royal priesthood, a holy nation, His own special people, that you may proclaim the praises of Him who called you out of darkness into His marvelous light;* ¹⁰*who once were not a people but are now the people of God, who had not obtained mercy but now have obtained mercy.*

EXPLORATION

1. How can we grow in our faith?

2. Why does Scripture call us "living stones"? To what positive traits does the term refer?

3. List several characteristics of Christ as the cornerstone.

4. How could Christ cause someone to stumble?

5. What special role has God given to us because we are Christians?

INSPIRATION

Can you still remember? Are you still in love with Him? . . . Remember Jesus. Before you remember anything, remember Him. If you forget anything, don't forget Him.

Oh, but how quickly we forget. So much happens through the years. So many changes within. So many alterations without. And, somewhere, back there, we leave Him. We don't turn away from Him . . . we just don't take Him with us. Assignments come. Promotions come. Budgets are made. Kids are born, and the Christ . . . the Christ is forgotten.

Has it been a while since you stared at the heavens in speechless amazement? Has it been a while since you realized God's divinity and your carnality?

If it has, then you need to know something. He is still there. He hasn't left. Under all those papers and books and reports and years. In the midst of all those voices and faces and memories and pictures, He is still there. (From *Six Hours One Friday* by Max Lucado)

REACTION

6. Think about the enthusiasm and commitment you had for Christ when you first became his follower. Why is that level of enthusiasm and commitment difficult to maintain?

7. How can we rekindle our first love for Jesus?

8. Why were we chosen to be God's people (v. 9)?

9. How can you determine whether Jesus is the cornerstone on which your life is built?

10. List some ways your daily life is different because of your relationship with Jesus. As the cornerstone, how does he define the shape of your life?

11. How does this passage reaffirm your sense of worth and value in God's eyes?

LIFE LESSONS

The purpose of the cornerstone in a building was to establish the lines. This rock had to be square and plumb because the rest of the building took its cues from the first block. Jesus may be a stumbling block for those who don't believe. But for us, he serves as the solid base for our lives. If we try to construct our lives without reference to him, we will fail. If our lives are anchored to him and oriented to him, the winds and storms of life will not destroy what we've built. All the other complimentary terms used to describe us in this passage relate directly to our relationship with Jesus. We are called these names because of him and what he has done for us.

DEVOTION

God, forgive us for the times we have left you behind in our struggle to get ahead. Forgive us for forgetting who you are and what you have done for us. We know that you have been there—always waiting, always hoping, and always ready to forgive. May we understand what it means to make you the cornerstone of our lives.

For more Bible passages on Christ, the cornerstone, see Psalm 118:21–24; Matthew 21:42–43; Acts 4:10–12; Ephesians 2:19–22.

To complete the books of 1 & 2 Peter during this twelve-part study, read 1 Peter 2:1–10.

JOURNALING

How would I compare my commitment to Christ when I first believed to my commitment now?

LESSON FOUR

FOLLOWING JESUS' EXAMPLE

MAX
LUCADO

REFLECTION

Some people make an impression on us because we can't imagine ever being like them. Others challenge us, by the very quality of their lives, to be like them. Think of a fellow believer whom you greatly admire. In what ways does that person's life challenge you? How would you like to model your life after that person's example? Why?

SITUATION

Christianity swept like wildfire through the ranks of the upper/middle class and slaves alike in the Roman Empire. The sources of suffering for these early Christians came from the world in general, from the government, or from harsh masters. Peter gave his readers wise counsel regarding their behavior and responses in social structures that were frequently unjust. They needed to know how to follow Jesus' example.

OBSERVATION

Read 1 Peter 2:11–25 from the NCV or the NKJV.

NCV

11Dear friends, you are like foreigners and strangers in this world. I beg you to avoid the evil things your bodies want to do that fight against your soul. 12People who do not believe are living all around you and might say that you are doing wrong. Live such good lives that they will see the good things you do and will give glory to God on the day when Christ comes again.

13For the Lord's sake, yield to the people who have authority in this world: the king, who is the highest authority, 14and the leaders who are sent by him to punish those who do wrong and to praise those who do right. 15It is God's desire that by doing good you should stop foolish people from saying stupid things about you. 16Live as free people, but do not use your freedom as an excuse to do evil. Live as servants of God. 17Show respect for all people: Love the brothers and sisters of God's family, respect God, honor the king.

¹⁸*Slaves, yield to the authority of your masters with all respect, not only those who are good and kind, but also those who are dishonest.* ¹⁹*A person might have to suffer even when it is unfair, but if he thinks of God and stands the pain, God is pleased.* ²⁰*If you are beaten for doing wrong, there is no reason to praise you for being patient in your punishment. But if you suffer for doing good, and you are patient, then God is pleased.* ²¹*This is what you were called to do, because Christ suffered for you and gave you an example to follow. So you should do as he did.*

²²*"He had never sinned,*

and he had never lied."

²³*People insulted Christ, but he did not insult them in return. Christ suffered, but he did not threaten. He let God, the One who judges rightly, take care of him.* ²⁴*Christ carried our sins in his body on the cross so we would stop living for sin and start living for what is right. And you are healed because of his wounds.* ²⁵*You were like sheep that wandered away, but now you have come back to the Shepherd and Protector of your souls.*

NKJV

¹¹*Beloved, I beg you as sojourners and pilgrims, abstain from fleshly lusts which war against the soul,* ¹²*having your conduct honorable among the Gentiles, that when they speak against you as evildoers, they may, by your good works which they observe, glorify God in the day of visitation.*

¹³*Therefore submit yourselves to every ordinance of man for the Lord's sake, whether to the king as supreme,* ¹⁴*or to governors, as to those who are sent by him for the punishment of evildoers and for the praise of those who do good.* ¹⁵*For this is the will of God, that by doing good you may put to silence the ignorance of foolish men—* ¹⁶*as free, yet not using liberty as a cloak for vice, but as bondservants of God.* ¹⁷*Honor all people. Love the brotherhood. Fear God. Honor the king.*

¹⁸*Servants, be submissive to your masters with all fear, not only to the good and gentle, but also to the harsh.* ¹⁹*For this is commendable, if because of conscience toward God one endures grief, suffering wrongfully.* ²⁰*For what credit is it if, when you are beaten for your faults, you take it patiently? But when you do good and suffer, if you take it patiently, this is commendable before God.* ²¹*For to this you were called, because Christ also suffered for us, leaving us an example, that you should follow His steps:*

²²*"Who committed no sin,*

Nor was deceit found in His mouth";

²³*who, when He was reviled, did not revile in return; when He suffered, He did not threaten, but committed Himself to Him who judges righteously;* ²⁴*who Himself bore our sins in His own body on the tree, that we, having died to sins, might live for righteousness—by whose stripes you were healed.* ²⁵*For you were like sheep going astray, but have now returned to the Shepherd and Overseer of your souls.*

EXPLORATION

1. Why didn't Jesus feel any need to seek revenge?

2. Why is it important for us to lead good lives, even in difficult circumstances?

3. Why should we yield to authorities?

4. What happens when believers endure suffering for doing good?

5. What can we learn from Jesus about responding to unfair treatment?

INSPIRATION

The disciples are annoyed. As Jesus sits in silence, they grow more smug. "Send her away," they demand. The spotlight is put on Jesus. He looks at the disciples, then looks at the woman. And what follows is one of the most intriguing dialogues in the New Testament.

"I was sent only to the lost sheep of Israel," he says.

"Lord, help me!"

"It is not right to take the children's bread and toss it to their dogs," he answers.

"But even the dogs eat the crumbs that fall from their masters' tables," she responds.

Is Jesus being rude? Is he worn-out? Is he frustrated? Is he calling this woman a dog? How do we explain this dialogue? . . .

Could it be that Jesus' tongue is poking his cheek? Could it be that he and the woman are engaging in satirical banter? Is it wry exchange in which God's unlimited grace is being highlighted? Could Jesus be so delighted to have found one who is not bartering with a religious system or proud of a heritage that he can't resist a bit of satire?

He knows he can heal her daughter. He knows he isn't bound by a plan. He knows her heart is good. So he decides to engage in a humorous moment with a faithful woman. In essence, here's what they said:

"Now, you know that God only cares about Jews," he says smiling.

And when she catches on, she volleys back, "But your bread is so precious, I'll be happy to eat the crumbs."

In a spirit of exuberance, he bursts out, "Never have I seen such faith! Your daughter is healed."

This story does not portray a contemptuous God. It portrays a willing One who delights in a sincere seeker.

Aren't you glad he does? (From *In the Eye of the Storm* by Max Lucado)

REACTION

6. The woman who approached Jesus in the quote from *In the Eye of the Storm* didn't take offense at Jesus' apparent refusal, as mistreatment. How do you tend to react when others hurt or mistreat you? How does this woman illustrate a wider idea of the kind of response to setbacks that pleases Jesus?

7. In what way does Christ's example affect the way you view your problems and pain?

8. How can our emotional wounds interfere with our spiritual growth?

9. In what circumstances is it tempting to retaliate?

10. When has God helped you forgive someone who hurt you deeply?

11. How can you fight the urge to get back at people who mistreat you?

LIFE LESSONS

Following Jesus' example when responding to mistreatment can seriously cramp our style. The problem isn't with Jesus' worthiness as an example, or the importance of following him, but that our "style" is made up of selfishness, pride, and personal agenda. In the laboratory of life, God wants to produce Jesus' character in us. In order to do so, he's not nearly as concerned with what happens to us as with how we respond. Following Jesus' example will take everything we have.

DEVOTION

Father, sometimes the urge to seek revenge seems too strong to resist. Even though we have experienced your great mercy and love, we refuse to extend your grace to others. Forgive us, Father, for choosing to retaliate instead of forgive. Remind us of how you dealt with injustice and unfairness when you were on earth, and give us the strength to follow your example.

For more Bible passages on following Jesus' example, see John 8:12; 12:26; 13:15; 1 Corinthians 11:1; Ephesians 5:1–2; 1 Thessalonians 1:6.

To complete the books of 1 & 2 Peter during this twelve-part study, read 1 Peter 2:11–25.

JOURNALING

Whom do I need to forgive? How can I follow Jesus' example of love in this relationship?

HOLY LIVING

MAX
LUCADO

REFLECTION

In this passage, Peter talks about living from the inside out. Consider someone you know who displays inner strength or inner beauty. How do you define these things? What habits or disciplines help develop inner strength and beauty?

SITUATION

Peter followed up the points about general submission for believers that we reviewed in the last lesson with some teaching on the narrower relationship of marriage. The depth of commitment to following Jesus isn't measured by how we perform in casual and shallow exchanges with people as much as it is measured by how that commitment affects our central relationships. Does Jesus have the last word on how we treat our husbands or wives?

OBSERVATION

Read 1 Peter 3:1–7 from the NCV or the NKJV.

NCV

¹In the same way, you wives should yield to your husbands. Then, if some husbands do not obey God's teaching, they will be persuaded to believe without anyone's saying a word to them. They will be persuaded by the way their wives live. ²Your husbands will see the pure lives you live with your respect for God. ³It is not fancy hair, gold jewelry, or fine clothes that should make you beautiful. ⁴No, your beauty should come from within you—the beauty of a gentle and quiet spirit that will never be destroyed and is very precious to God. ⁵In this same way the holy women who lived long ago and followed God made themselves beautiful, yielding to their own husbands. ⁶Sarah obeyed Abraham, her husband, and called him her master. And you women are true children of Sarah if you always do what is right and are not afraid.

⁷In the same way, you husbands should live with your wives in an understanding way, since they are weaker than you. But show them respect, because God gives them the same blessing he gives you—the grace that gives true life. Do this so that nothing will stop your prayers.

NKJV

¹Wives, likewise, be submissive to your own husbands, that even if some do not obey the word, they, without a word, may be won by the conduct of their wives, ²when they observe your chaste conduct accompanied by fear. ³Do not let your adornment be merely outward—arranging the hair, wearing gold, or putting on fine apparel—⁴rather let it be the hidden person of the heart, with the incorruptible beauty of a gentle and quiet spirit, which is very precious in the sight of God. ⁵For in this manner, in former times, the holy women who trusted in God also adorned themselves, being submissive to their own husbands, ⁶as Sarah obeyed Abraham, calling him lord, whose daughters you are if you do good and are not afraid with any terror.

⁷Husbands, likewise, dwell with them with understanding, giving honor to the wife, as to the weaker vessel, and as being heirs together of the grace of life, that your prayers may not be hindered.

EXPLORATION

1. How can believing wives win their unbelieving husbands to Christ?

2. Why is inner beauty precious to God?

3. List some ways we can cultivate inner beauty.

4. What can we learn from women like Sarah who lived long ago?

5. In what ways do others benefit when believers live holy, pure lives?

INSPIRATION

Would you do what Jesus did? He swapped a spotless castle for a grimy stable. He exchanged the worship of angels for the company of killers. He could hold the universe in his palm but gave it up to float in the womb of a maiden.

If you were God, would you sleep on straw, nurse from a breast, and be clothed in a diaper? I wouldn't, but Christ did.

If you knew that only a few would care that you came, would you still come? If you knew that those you loved would laugh in your face, would you still care? If you knew that the tongues you made would mock you, the mouths you made would spit at you, the hands you made would crucify you, would you still make them? Christ did. Would you regard the immobile and invalid more important than yourself? Jesus did.

He humbled himself. He went from commanding angels to sleeping in the straw. From holding stars to clutching Mary's finger. The palm that held the universe took the nail of a soldier.

Why? Because that's what love does. It puts the beloved before itself. Your soul was more important than his blood. Your eternal life was more important than his earthly life. Your place in heaven was more important to him than his place in heaven, so he gave up his so you could have yours. He loves you that much, and because he loves you, you are of prime importance to him . . .

Want to love others as God has loved you? Come thirsty. Drink deeply of God's love for you, and ask him to fill your heart with a love worth giving. (From *A Love Worth Giving* by Max Lucado)

REACTION

6. How are humility and holiness related? How can you demonstrate humility and love in your marriage?

7. Why is it important to realize that becoming holy is a process, not a one-time event?

8. What is God's part and what is our responsibility in the sanctification process?

9. Why do we pay more attention to what people *do* than to what they say?

10. List some ways we focus more on enhancing our outward appearance than developing our inner character.

11. What about our lives will attract people to Christ?

LIFE LESSONS

The word *crucible* carries a double meaning. It is a container designed to take the extreme heat of molten metal. It is also used to describe a severe test. Marriage functions like a relationship crucible. The wedding vows create a container for the high temperatures of relationship development. The holy lives that God wants in his children can be developed in the crucible of marriage, but the process isn't easy. It requires commitment, forgiveness, submission (to God and one another), and continued faithfulness through heat and cool. The results are worth the efforts required.

DEVOTION

Father, we want to be holy, but we are weak and prone to sin. Manifest your holiness in us, especially in our closest relationships. Help us to surrender our selfish desires to your perfect will. Teach us what it means to live by your Spirit, not our flesh. Persuade others to believe in you through our lives.

For more Bible passages on holy living, see Leviticus 11:44–45; 1 Corinthians 1:2, 30; 1 Thessalonians 4:3–7; 2 Timothy 1:8–9; Hebrews 10:10–14; 1 Peter 1:14–16; 2 Peter 3:11.

To complete the books of 1 & 2 Peter during this twelve-part study, read 1 Peter 3:1–7.

JOURNALING

How can I pay attention to developing inner character? What do I need to surrender to God?

LESSON SIX

LOVING
PEOPLE

MAX
LUCADO

REFLECTION

Describe a time when someone demonstrated Christ's love to you in a practical way. Think about what it cost the person to help you. In what ways has that gesture affected the way you notice and respond to other people's needs?

SITUATION

Not only did Peter want to encourage his readers in their active witness for Christ; he also wanted them to be ready to explain what they believed. Many of the lifestyle choices described up until this point would tend to create curiosity in the minds of observers. People don't submit or cooperate in difficult situations unless they have hope. When people ask us about our hope, Peter says, be ready to explain it clearly.

OBSERVATION

Read 1 Peter 3:8—22 from the NCV or the NKJV.

NCV

8Finally, all of you should be in agreement, understanding each other, loving each other as family, being kind and humble. 9Do not do wrong to repay a wrong, and do not insult to repay an insult. But repay with a blessing, because you yourselves were called to do this so that you might receive a blessing. 10The Scripture says,

> *"A person must do these things*
>
> *to enjoy life and have many happy days.*
>
> *He must not say evil things,*
>
> *and he must not tell lies.*
>
> *11He must stop doing evil and do good.*
>
> *He must look for peace and work for it.*
>
> *12The Lord sees the good people*
>
> *and listens to their prayers.*
>
> *But the Lord is against*
>
> *those who do evil."*

13If you are trying hard to do good, no one can really hurt you. 14But even if you suffer for doing right, you are blessed.

> *"Don't be afraid of what they fear;*
>
> *do not dread those things."*

15But respect Christ as the holy Lord in your hearts. Always be ready to answer everyone who asks you to explain about the hope you have, 16but answer in a gentle way and with respect. Keep a clear conscience so that those who speak evil of your good life in Christ will be made ashamed. 17It is better to suffer for doing good than for doing wrong if that is what God wants. 18Christ himself suffered for sins once. He was not guilty, but he suffered for those who are guilty to bring you to God. His body was killed, but he was made alive in the spirit. 19And in the spirit he went and preached to the spirits in prison 20who refused to obey God long ago in the time of Noah. God was waiting patiently for them while Noah was building the boat. Only a few people—eight in all—were saved by water. 21And that water is like baptism that now saves you—not the washing of dirt from the body, but the promise made to God from a good conscience. And this is because Jesus Christ was raised from the dead. 22Now Jesus has gone into heaven and is at God's right side ruling over angels, authorities, and powers.

NKJV

⁸*Finally, all of you be of one mind, having compassion for one another; love as brothers, be tenderhearted, be courteous; ⁹not returning evil for evil or reviling for reviling, but on the contrary blessing, knowing that you were called to this, that you may inherit a blessing. ¹⁰For*

> *"He who would love life*
>
> *And see good days,*
>
> *Let him refrain his tongue from evil,*
>
> *And his lips from speaking deceit.*
>
> *¹¹Let him turn away from evil and do good;*
>
> *Let him seek peace and pursue it.*
>
> *¹²For the eyes of the LORD are on the righteous,*
>
> *And His ears are open to their prayers;*
>
> *But the face of the LORD is against those who do evil."*

¹³*And who is he who will harm you if you become followers of what is good? ¹⁴But even if you should suffer for righteousness' sake, you are blessed. "And do not be afraid of their threats, nor be troubled." ¹⁵But sanctify the Lord God in your hearts, and always be ready to give a defense to everyone who asks you a reason for the hope that is in you, with meekness and fear; ¹⁶having a good conscience, that when they defame you as evildoers, those who revile your good conduct in Christ may be ashamed. ¹⁷For it is better, if it is the will of God, to suffer for doing good than for doing evil.*

¹⁸*For Christ also suffered once for sins, the just for the unjust, that He might bring us to God, being put to death in the flesh but made alive by the Spirit, ¹⁹by whom also He went and preached to the spirits in prison, ²⁰who formerly were disobedient, when once the Divine longsuffering waited in the days of Noah, while the ark was being prepared, in which a few, that is, eight souls, were saved through water. ²¹There is also an antitype which now saves us—baptism (not the removal of the filth of the flesh, but the answer of a good conscience toward God), through the resurrection of Jesus Christ, ²²who has gone into heaven and is at the right hand of God, angels and authorities and powers having been made subject to Him.*

EXPLORATION

1. How should we treat one another? In what ways has the church you attend been an example of Christian behavior in the community?

2. When is it most difficult to demonstrate a loving attitude toward others—even other Christians?

3. Describe the kind of person who enjoys life and pleases God.

4. Why is it better to suffer for doing good than for doing wrong?

5. What difference does Christ's resurrection make in how we treat others?

INSPIRATION

In our house we call 5:00 P.M. the piranha hour. That's the time of day when everyone wants a piece of Mom. Sara, the baby, is hungry. Andrea wants Mom to read her a book. Jenna wants help with her homework. And I—the ever-loving, eversensitive husband—want Denalyn to drop everything and talk to me about my day.

When is your piranha hour? When do people in your world demand much and offer little?

Every boss has had a day in which the requests outnumber the results. There's not a businessperson alive who hasn't groaned as an armada of assignments docks at his or her desk. For the teacher, the piranha hour often begins when the first student enters and ends when the last student leaves.

Piranha hours. Parents have them, bosses endure them, secretaries dread them, teachers are besieged by them, and Jesus taught us how to live through them successfully.

When hands extended and voices demanded, Jesus responded with love. He did so because the code within him disarmed the alarm. The code is worth noting: "People are precious." (From *In the Eye of the Storm* by Max Lucado)

REACTION

6. When is your "piranha hour"?

7. How can we find the strength to love people, even when they have nothing to give in return?

8. In what way can you remind yourself of Christ's example the next time you feel overwhelmed by the demands of others?

9. What kinds of issues create tension and conflict between believers?

10. What practical steps can we take to promote harmony in the body of Christ?

11. What does it mean to work for peace?

LIFE LESSONS

The Christian life is often counter to human instincts. In our "natural" state we humans want to return evil for evil and reviling for reviling. We believe that what goes around comes around, and we want to give it an extra shove when it goes by us! If we're going to follow Jesus, though, we can't follow our natural instincts. If we are going to obey Jesus' command to love others, we have to ignore our inclination to have things our way. Jesus goes beyond his role as our example—he also empowers us to love beyond what we could ever do in our own strength.

DEVOTION

Father, when we feel incapable of showing your love to others, when we have nothing left to give, we pray that you would fill us with your grace. During those dry, dark times, Father, we ask that you would give us the strength to love sacrificially. Teach us how to love as you loved. May your mercy and compassion overflow from our hearts to others.

For more Bible passages on loving people, see Matthew 5:43–48; 22:38–40; John 13:34–35; Romans 12:9–10; 1 Corinthians 13:1–13; Galatians 5:13–14; Colossians 3:14; 1 Thessalonians 4:9–10; Hebrews 10:24; 1 Peter 1:22; 1 John 3:11, 16–18; 4:7–21; 2 John 5–6.

To complete the books of 1 & 2 Peter during this twelve-part study, read 1 Peter 3:8–22.

JOURNALING

What can I value about someone I find hard to love?

LESSON SEVEN

JOYFUL
SERVICE

MAX
LUCADO

REFLECTION

The joy that emerges from serving others is often unexpected, even surprising. Think of a time when you found great joy in serving in your church or community. What made that experience joyful for you? When have you experienced joy in using your spiritual gift to serve someone else?

SITUATION

The two sections in this passage reveal a vivid contrast between the old life and our new life in Christ. The two lives are not compatible. Peter warned of the consequences that would follow the old life, and encouraged his readers to devote themselves to living for God's glory.

OBSERVATION

Read 1 Peter 4:1–11 from the NCV or the NKJV.

NCV

¹Since Christ suffered while he was in his body, strengthen yourselves with the same way of thinking Christ had. The person who has suffered in the body is finished with sin. ²Strengthen yourselves so that you will live here on earth doing what God wants, not the evil things people want. ³In the past you wasted too much time doing what nonbelievers enjoy. You were guilty of sexual sins, evil desires, drunkenness, wild and drunken parties, and hateful idol worship. ⁴Nonbelievers think it is strange that you do not do the many wild and wasteful things they do, so they insult you. ⁵But they will have to explain this to God, who is ready to judge the living and the dead. ⁶For this reason the Good News was preached to those who are now dead. Even though they were judged like all people, the Good News was preached to them so they could live in the spirit as God lives.

⁷The time is near when all things will end. So think clearly and control yourselves so you will be able to pray. ⁸Most importantly, love each other deeply, because love will cause many sins to be forgiven. ⁹Open your homes to each other, without complaining. ¹⁰Each of you has received a gift to use to serve others. Be good servants of God's various gifts of grace. ¹¹Anyone who speaks should speak words from God. Anyone who serves should serve with the strength God gives so that in everything God will be praised through Jesus Christ. Power and glory belong to him forever and ever. Amen.

NKJV

¹Therefore, since Christ suffered for us in the flesh, arm yourselves also with the same mind, for he who has suffered in the flesh has ceased from sin, ²that he no longer should live the rest of his time in the flesh for the lusts of men, but for the will of God. ³For we have spent enough of our past lifetime in doing the will of the Gentiles—when we walked in lewdness, lusts, drunkenness, revelries, drinking parties, and abominable idolatries. ⁴In regard to these, they think it strange that you do not run with them in the same flood of dissipation, speaking evil of you. ⁵They will give an account to Him who is ready to judge the living and the dead. ⁶For this reason the gospel was preached also to those who are dead, that they might be judged according to men in the flesh, but live according to God in the spirit.

⁷But the end of all things is at hand; therefore be serious and watchful in your prayers. ⁸And above all things have fervent love for one another, for "love will cover a multitude of sins." ⁹Be hospitable to one another without grumbling. ¹⁰As each one has received a gift, minister it to one another, as good stewards of the manifold grace of God. ¹¹If anyone speaks, let him speak as the oracles of God. If anyone ministers, let him do it as with the ability which God supplies, that in all things God may be glorified through Jesus Christ, to whom belong the glory and the dominion forever and ever. Amen.

EXPLORATION

1. How can we strengthen ourselves and develop our gifts?

2. According to Peter, what are the results of loving others?

3. What does it mean to be gifted by God?

4. Think of someone who, in your opinion, used his or her giftedness to serve God. Describe that person.

5. What is the purpose of the gifts and talents God gives us?

INSPIRATION

I recently read a story of a woman who for years was married to a harsh husband. Each day he would leave her a list of chores to complete before he returned at the end of the day. "Clean the yard. Stack the firewood. Wash the windows . . . "

If she didn't complete the tasks, she would be greeted with his explosive anger. But even if she did complete the list, he was never satisfied; he would always find inadequacies in her work.

After several years, the husband passed away. Some time later she remarried, this time to a man who lavished her with tenderness and adoration.

One day, while going through a box of old papers, the wife discovered one of her first husband's lists. And as she read the sheet, a realization caused a tear of joy to splash on the paper.

"I'm still doing all these things, and no one has to tell me. I do it because I love him."

That is the unique characteristic of the new kingdom. Its subjects don't work *in order to* go to heaven; they work because they *are* going to heaven. Arrogance and fear are replaced with gratitude and joy. (From *The Applause of Heaven* by Max Lucado)

REACTION

6. What usually motivates you to serve?

7. In what way does the promise of eternal life impact your attitude toward serving?

8. How can a person find true joy in serving others?

9. What blessings have you received from serving others?

10. How can you depend on God to help you serve, instead of relying on your own strength?

11. In what tangible way can you express your gratitude to God today?

LIFE LESSONS

Serving is easy when you are motivated. We are motivated to love and serve because of Christ's suffering for us. Since he did so much for us, when none of us deserved it, how can we not do all we can for him? Our best efforts at service represent the highest form of gratitude we can express to God for his gift of love and eternal life.

DEVOTION

Father, give us a deeper appreciation for what you have done for us and new enthusiasm for serving you. Show us how to extend your love to others. Most importantly, Father, help us to turn to you for wisdom, strength, and perseverance. We give you all the glory for what you will accomplish through us.

For more Bible passages on serving, see Deuteronomy 10:12; 13:4; Joshua 22:5; Psalm 100:2; Matthew 20:26–28; Romans 12:11; 2 Corinthians 9:12; Galatians 5:13; Ephesians 4:11–13; 6:6–8; Colossians 3:23–24.

To complete the books of 1 & 2 Peter during this twelve-part study, read 1 Peter 4:1–11.

JOURNALING

What are my gifts, and how can I use them to serve others?

TRUSTING GOD THROUGH TRIALS

MAX LUCADO

REFLECTION

Talking about God's faithfulness as a general concept is quite different from experiencing it in our lives. Think of a time when God proved his trustworthiness to you in a unique way. It may have been in a difficult situation or in a happy situation. How did that experience stretch your faith?

SITUATION

Peter reminded his beloved brothers and sisters in Christ that hard times are not always a mystery. Sometimes we experience difficulty because we have done something to deserve it. Consequences for sin are real. Peter didn't want them to think they were exempt from sin or from suffering. But when we suffer for Christ's sake, God uses those trials for our benefit, as well as to bring glory to himself.

OBSERVATION

Read 1 Peter 4:12—19 from the NCV or the NKJV.

NCV

¹²My friends, do not be surprised at the terrible trouble which now comes to test you. Do not think that something strange is happening to you. ¹³But be happy that you are sharing in Christ's sufferings so that you will be happy and full of joy when Christ comes again in glory. ¹⁴When people insult you because you follow Christ, you are blessed, because the glorious Spirit, the Spirit of God, is with you. ¹⁵Do not suffer for murder, theft, or any other crime, nor because you trouble other people. ¹⁶But if you suffer because you are a Christian, do not be ashamed. Praise God because you wear that name. ¹⁷It is time for judgment to begin with God's family. And if that judging begins with us, what will happen to those people who do not obey the Good News of God?

¹⁸"If it is very hard for a good person to be saved,

the wicked person and the sinner will surely be lost!"

¹⁹So those who suffer as God wants should trust their souls to the faithful Creator as they continue to do what is right.

NKJV

¹²Beloved, do not think it strange concerning the fiery trial which is to try you, as though some strange thing happened to you; ¹³but rejoice to the extent that you partake of Christ's sufferings, that when His glory is revealed, you may also be glad with exceeding joy. ¹⁴If you are reproached for the name of Christ, blessed are you, for the Spirit of glory and of God rests upon you. On their part He is blasphemed, but on your part He is glorified. ¹⁵But let none of you suffer as a murderer, a thief, an evildoer, or as a busybody in other people's matters. ¹⁶Yet if anyone suffers as a Christian, let him not be ashamed, but let him glorify God in this matter.

¹⁷For the time has come for judgment to begin at the house of God; and if it begins with us first, what will be the end of those who do not obey the gospel of God? ¹⁸Now

"If the righteous one is scarcely saved,

Where will the ungodly and the sinner appear?"

¹⁹Therefore let those who suffer according to the will of God commit their souls to Him in doing good, as to a faithful Creator.

EXPLORATION

1. In what ways does God test us? What are his purposes?

2. How can we share in Christ's sufferings?

3. Why should we rejoice in difficult circumstances?

4. What kind of suffering does God want us to avoid, and what kind does he want us to welcome?

5. In what way can suffering be a blessing?

INSPIRATION

Is there anything more frail than a bruised reed? Look at the bruised reed at the water's edge. A once slender and tall stalk of sturdy river grass, it is now bowed and bent.

Are you a bruised reed? Was it so long ago that you stood so tall, so proud? You were upright and sturdy, nourished by the waters and rooted in the riverbed of confidence.

Then something happened. You were bruised . . .

> by harsh words
>
> by a friend's anger
>
> by a spouse's betrayal
>
> by your own failure
>
> by religion's rigidity.

And you were wounded, bent ever so slightly. Your hollow reed, once erect, now stooped, and hidden in the bulrush.

And the smoldering wick on the candle. Is there anything closer to death than a smoldering wick? Once aflame, now flickering and failing. Still warm from yesterday's passion, but no fire. Not yet cold, but far from hot. Was it that long ago you blazed with faith? Remember how you illuminated the path?

Then came the wind . . . the cold wind, the harsh wind. They said your ideas were foolish. They told you your dreams were too lofty. They scolded you for challenging the time-tested. The constant wind wore down upon you. Oh, you stood strong for a moment (or maybe a lifetime), but the endless blast whipped your flickering flame, leaving you one pinch away from darkness.

The bruised reed and the smoldering wick. Society knows what to do with you. The world has a place for the beaten. The world will break you off; the world will snuff you out.

But the artists of Scripture proclaim that God won't. Painted on canvas after canvas is the tender touch of a Creator who has a special place for the bruised and weary of the world. A God who is the friend of the wounded heart. A God who is the keeper of your dreams. (From *He Still Moves Stones* by Max Lucado)

REACTION

6. What hope is there for those of us who are emotionally wounded?

7. What can we do to develop a faith that will withstand pressure and persecution?

8. Is there any way God has used pain and suffering in your life for good? How?

9. In what ways have you suffered because of your faith in Jesus Christ?

10. Why should we not be surprised when we experience troubles?

11. In practical terms, how can you trust God to help you through difficult times in your life?

LIFE LESSONS

Life has a way of riding roughshod over our expectations, ending in disappointment. Peter doesn't tell us to avoid expectations; he simply gives us some guidelines about what to expect. One wise expectation involves the fact that God can use any circumstance to bring about good for us. Even when the hardship is clearly our fault. That's why we must always "trust our souls to our faithful Creator." He is trustworthy.

DEVOTION

Father, you never said that this life would be easy. Instead, you warned us to expect pain and troubles. But you also promised that you would be with us. O Father, teach us to rely on you, so that we can withstand the struggles and storms that come our way. And even when we cannot understand why you are allowing us to suffer, help us to trust you.

For more Bible passages on trials, see Acts 5:41; Romans 5:3; 8:17–18; 2 Corinthians 1:5–7; Philippians 1:29; 3:10; 1 Thessalonians 3:3–4; 2 Thessalonians 1:3–4; 2 Timothy 1:8; Hebrews 12:10–11; James 1:2–4; 1 Peter 1:6–7; 2:19–21.

To complete the books of 1 & 2 Peter during this twelve-part study, read 1 Peter 4:12–19.

JOURNALING

How can I thank God for the trials in my life?

LESSON NINE

HUMILITY

MAX
LUCADO

REFLECTION

Humility is a most illusive personal quality. It suddenly vanishes just at the moment you realize you've achieved it! We rarely list "humble" on our résumés, but we hope others might consider including that word in describing us. It takes the observation of others to confirm any progress in humility. Think of a respected Christian leader in your community. How has that person set a good example of humility for others to follow?

SITUATION

Peter closed his first letter with a special challenge to the leaders and to young people. He was thinking about present and future leadership. He knew that the church has a fearsome but defeated enemy, who seeks to destroy. But there is overwhelming reason for hope in Christ!

OBSERVATION

Read 1 Peter 5:1–14 from the NCV or the NKJV.

NCV

¹Now I have something to say to the elders in your group. I also am an elder. I have seen Christ's sufferings, and I will share in the glory that will be shown to us. I beg you to ²shepherd God's flock, for whom you are responsible. Watch over them because you want to, not because you are forced. That is how God wants it. Do it because you are happy to serve, not because you want money. ³Do not be like a ruler over people you are responsible for, but be good examples to them. ⁴Then when Christ, the Chief Shepherd, comes, you will get a glorious crown that will never lose its beauty.

⁵In the same way, younger people should be willing to be under older people. And all of you should be very humble with each other.

"God is against the proud,

but he gives grace to the humble."

⁶Be humble under God's powerful hand so he will lift you up when the right time comes. ⁷Give all your worries to him, because he cares about you.

⁸Control yourselves and be careful! The devil, your enemy, goes around like a roaring lion looking for someone to eat. ⁹Refuse to give in to him, by standing strong in your faith. You know that your Christian family all over the world is having the same kinds of suffering.

¹⁰And after you suffer for a short time, God, who gives all grace, will make everything right. He will make you strong and support you and keep you from falling. He called you to share in his glory in Christ, a glory that will continue forever. ¹¹All power is his forever and ever. Amen.

¹²I wrote this short letter with the help of Silas, who I know is a faithful brother in Christ. I wrote to encourage you and to tell you that this is the true grace of God. Stand strong in that grace.

¹³The church in Babylon, who was chosen like you, sends you greetings. Mark, my son in Christ, also greets you. ¹⁴Give each other a kiss of Christian love when you meet.

Peace to all of you who are in Christ.

NKJV

¹The elders who are among you I exhort, I who am a fellow elder and a witness of the sufferings of Christ, and also a partaker of the glory that will be revealed: ²Shepherd the flock of God which is among you, serving as overseers, not by compulsion but willingly, not for dishonest gain but eagerly; ³nor as being lords over those entrusted to you, but being examples to the flock; ⁴and when the Chief Shepherd appears, you will receive the crown of glory that does not fade away.

⁵Likewise you younger people, submit yourselves to your elders. Yes, all of you be submissive to one another, and be clothed with humility, for

"God resists the proud,

But gives grace to the humble."

⁶Therefore humble yourselves under the mighty hand of God, that He may exalt you in due time, ⁷casting all your care upon Him, for He cares for you.

⁸Be sober, be vigilant; because your adversary the devil walks about like a roaring lion, seeking whom he may devour. ⁹Resist him, steadfast in the faith, knowing that the same sufferings are experienced by your brotherhood in the world. ¹⁰But may the God of all grace, who called us to His eternal glory by Christ Jesus, after you have suffered a while, perfect, establish, strengthen, and settle you. ¹¹To Him be the glory and the dominion forever and ever. Amen.

¹²By Silvanus, our faithful brother as I consider him, I have written to you briefly, exhorting and testifying that this is the true grace of God in which you stand.

¹³She who is in Babylon, elect together with you, greets you; and so does Mark my son. ¹⁴Greet one another with a kiss of love.

Peace to you all who are in Christ Jesus. Amen.

EXPLORATION

1. List some responsibilities of church leaders. How have you exercised or experienced these personally?

2. In what way does a spirit of humility among believers benefit the church?

3. How does God reward the humble?

4. List some ways God helps us remain faithful to him.

5. What future can God's people anticipate?

INSPIRATION

Of all the times we see the bowing knees of Jesus, none is so precious as when he kneels before his disciples and washes their feet (see John 13:1–5).

It has been a long day. Jerusalem is packed with Passover guests, most of whom clamor for a glimpse of the Teacher. The spring sun is warm. The streets are dry. And the disciples are a long way from home. A splash of cool water would be refreshing.

The disciples enter, one by one, and take their places around the table. On the wall hangs a towel, and on the floor sits a pitcher and a basin. Any one of the disciples could volunteer for the job, but not one does.

After a few moments, Jesus stands and removes his outer garment. He wraps a servant's girdle around his waist, takes up the basin, and kneels before one of the disciples. He unlaces a sandal and gently lifts the foot and places it in the basin, covers it with water, and begins to bathe it. One by one, one grimy foot after another, Jesus works his way down the row.

In Jesus' day the washing of feet was a task reserved not just for servants but for the lowest of servants. Every circle has its pecking order, and the circle of household workers was no exception. The servant at the bottom of the totem pole was expected to be the one on his knees with the towel and the basin.

In this case the one with the towel and basin is the King of the universe. Hands that shaped the stars now wash away filth. Fingers that formed mountains now massage toes. And the one before whom all nations will one day kneel now kneels before his disciples. Hours before his own death, Jesus' concern is singular. He wants his disciples to know how much he loves them. More than removing dirt, Jesus is removing doubt. (From *Just Like Jesus Devotional* by Max Lucado)

REACTION

6. Besides washing the disciples' feet, in what other ways did Jesus demonstrate humility?

7. Why is it difficult to be humble? How can we protect ourselves from the sin of pride?

8. Think of one person to whom you can be accountable in your Christian walk. How can he or she best help you?

9. Why is pride a temptation for church leaders?

10. List some signs or evidences of pride.

11. In what practical ways can we humble ourselves?

LIFE LESSONS

A starting point in practicing humility comes when we realize that there's no such thing as a humble feeling. There are humble *actions*, and most of them go unnoticed by anyone else. If we demand to be noticed, we're not acting in humility. This is why Jesus' example has such power. When we are imitating him, we are carrying out humble actions. These will almost always involve service.

DEVOTION

Father, thank you for sending your Son to earth to show us how to become servant leaders. Give us the grace to follow his example. Open our eyes to the blind spots in our lives, and help us root out any trace of pride. And Father, thank you for your promise that, at the right time, you will lift up the humble.

For more Bible passages on humility, see Proverbs 11:2; 15:33; Zephaniah 2:3; Luke 14:11; Ephesians 4:2; Philippians 2:3; Colossians 3:12; James 4:10.

To complete the books of 1 & 2 Peter during this twelve-part study, read 1 Peter 5:1–14.

JOURNALING

Where in my life do I need more humility?

INTRODUCTION TO THE BOOK OF 2 PETER

If a friend warns you, it's one thing. If a doctor warns you, you listen. But if your friend is your doctor, you lean forward and take note.

My friend is my doctor. My doctor is my friend. Most of my physical exams are salted with friendly chatter and jokes. There have been occasions, however, when his tone gets solemn and his voice urgent.

"We're going to have to watch this, Max."

"You haven't been exercising, have you?"

"With your family's history, you have to watch your diet."

When it's a warning from a friend, you listen.

The second letter from Peter is a warning from a friend. His first letter was a warning about trials from without (persecution). His second caution is a warning about trials from within (heresy).

In this, the last letter we have from him, he urges Christians to be careful. Avoid shortsightedness (1:2–11). Be on guard for false teachers (2:1–22). And, most importantly, be vigilant against personal complacency, which will lead to a lazy faith.

The doctor's task is to detect concerns from within and urge you to take caution. Peter's task is the same. Heed his counsel.

LESSON TEN

SELF-
DISCIPLINE

MAX
LUCADO

REFLECTION

People have long practiced specific actions designed to sharpen spiritual aware-
ness, challenge bad habits, and create accelerated spiritual growth. These pat-
terns of behavior have been called "spiritual disciplines." Familiar disciplines,
such as prayer, Bible reading, and personal worship, have been pursued alongside
less familiar disciplines like fasting, silence, and study. What spiritual disciplines
have helped you the most in your Christian walk?

SITUATION

Peter was aware that his life would soon be over. He began this last letter with a
tribute to Jesus Christ. He wanted to convince his readers that as long as their
faith was focused on Jesus, they would have all they needed in order to meet any
challenge. He reminded them to keep growing, and add to their lives the "fruit"
of self-control, goodness, knowledge, and love.

OBSERVATION

Read 2 Peter 1:1—21 from the NCV or the NKJV.

NCV

¹From Simon Peter, a servant and apostle of Jesus Christ.

*To you who have received a faith as valuable as ours, because our God and Savior Jesus
Christ does what is right.*

*²Grace and peace be given to you more and more, because you truly know God and
Jesus our Lord.*

*³Jesus has the power of God, by which he has given us everything we need to live and to
serve God. We have these things because we know him. Jesus called us by his glory and
goodness. ⁴Through these he gave us the very great and precious promises. With these
gifts you can share in being like God, and the world will not ruin you with its evil desires.*

[5] *Because you have these blessings, do your best to add these things to your lives: to your faith, add goodness; and to your goodness, add knowledge;* [6]*and to your knowledge, add self-control; and to your self-control, add patience; and to your patience, add service for God;* [7]*and to your service for God, add kindness for your brothers and sisters in Christ; and to this kindness, add love.* [8]*If all these things are in you and are growing, they will help you to be useful and productive in your knowledge of our Lord Jesus Christ.* [9]*But anyone who does not have these things cannot see clearly. He is blind and has forgotten that he was made clean from his past sins.*

[10]*My brothers and sisters, try hard to be certain that you really are called and chosen by God. If you do all these things, you will never fall.* [11]*And you will be given a very great welcome into the eternal kingdom of our Lord and Savior Jesus Christ.*

[12]*You know these things, and you are very strong in the truth, but I will always help you remember them.* [13]*I think it is right for me to help you remember as long as I am in this body.* [14]*I know I must soon leave this body, as our Lord Jesus Christ has shown me.* [15]*I will try my best so that you may be able to remember these things even after I am gone.*

[16]*When we told you about the powerful coming of our Lord Jesus Christ, we were not telling just smart stories that someone invented. But we saw the greatness of Jesus with our own eyes.* [17]*Jesus heard the voice of God, the Greatest Glory, when he received honor and glory from God the Father. The voice said, "This is my Son, whom I love, and I am very pleased with him."* [18]*We heard that voice from heaven while we were with Jesus on the holy mountain.*

[19]*This makes us more sure about the message the prophets gave. It is good for you to follow closely what they said as you would follow a light shining in a dark place, until the day begins and the morning star rises in your hearts.* [20]*Most of all, you must understand this: No prophecy in the Scriptures ever comes from the prophet's own interpretation.* [21]*No prophecy ever came from what a person wanted to say, but people led by the Holy Spirit spoke words from God.*

NKJV

[1]*Simon Peter, a bondservant and apostle of Jesus Christ,*

To those who have obtained like precious faith with us by the righteousness of our God and Savior Jesus Christ:

[2]*Grace and peace be multiplied to you in the knowledge of God and of Jesus our Lord,* [3]*as His divine power has given to us all things that pertain to life and godliness, through the knowledge of Him who called us by glory and virtue,* [4]*by which have been given to us exceedingly great and precious promises, that through these you may be partakers of the divine nature, having escaped the corruption that is in the world through lust.*

[5]*But also for this very reason, giving all diligence, add to your faith virtue, to virtue knowledge,* [6]*to knowledge self-control, to self-control perseverance, to perseverance godliness,* [7]*to godliness brotherly kindness, and to brotherly kindness love.*

8For if these things are yours and abound, you will be neither barren nor unfruitful in the knowledge of our Lord Jesus Christ. 9For he who lacks these things is shortsighted, even to blindness, and has forgotten that he was cleansed from his old sins.

10Therefore, brethren, be even more diligent to make your call and election sure, for if you do these things you will never stumble; 11for so an entrance will be supplied to you abundantly into the everlasting kingdom of our Lord and Savior Jesus Christ.

12For this reason I will not be negligent to remind you always of these things, though you know and are established in the present truth. 13Yes, I think it is right, as long as I am in this tent, to stir you up by reminding you, 14knowing that shortly I must put off my tent, just as our Lord Jesus Christ showed me. 15Moreover I will be careful to ensure that you always have a reminder of these things after my decease.

16For we did not follow cunningly devised fables when we made known to you the power and coming of our Lord Jesus Christ, but were eyewitnesses of His majesty. 17For He received from God the Father honor and glory when such a voice came to Him from the Excellent Glory: "This is My beloved Son, in whom I am well pleased." 18And we heard this voice which came from heaven when we were with Him on the holy mountain.

19And so we have the prophetic word confirmed, which you do well to heed as a light that shines in a dark place, until the day dawns and the morning star rises in your hearts; 20knowing this first, that no prophecy of Scripture is of any private interpretation, 21for prophecy never came by the will of man, but holy men of God spoke as they were moved by the Holy Spirit.

EXPLORATION

1. What are the good things we have received from Jesus Christ?

2. List some character traits that we need to work on to instill them in our own lives.

3. Describe the process it takes to develop these character traits.

4. What confirms to us that we are called and chosen by God?

5. How can we trust what is recorded in Scripture?

INSPIRATION

Though he creates, God was never created. Though he makes, he was never made. Though he causes, he was never caused. Hence the psalmist's proclamation: "Before the mountains were born or you brought forth the earth and the world, from everlasting to everlasting you are God" (Ps. 90:2 NIV).

God is Yahweh—an unchanging God, an uncaused God, and an ungoverned God.

You and I are governed. The weather determines what we wear. The terrain tells us how to travel. Gravity dictates our speed, and health determines our strength. We may challenge these forces and alter them slightly, but we never remove them.

God—our Shepherd—doesn't check the weather; he makes it. He doesn't defy gravity; he created it. He isn't affected by health; he has no body. Jesus said, "God is spirit" (John 4:24 NIV). Since he has no body; he has no limitation—equally active in Cambodia as he is in Connecticut. "Where can I go to get away from your Spirit?" asked David. "Where can I run from you? If I go up to the heavens, you are there. If I lie down in the grave, you are there" (Ps. 139:7–8 NCV).

Unchanging. Uncaused. Ungoverned. These are only a fraction of God's qualities, but aren't they enough to give you a glimpse of your Father? Don't we need this kind of shepherd? Don't we need an unchanging shepherd?

When Lloyd Douglas, author of *The Robe* and other novels, attended college, he lived in a boardinghouse. A retired, wheelchair-bound music professor resided on the first floor. Each morning Douglas would stick his head in the door of the teacher's apartment and ask the same question, "Well, what's the good news?" The old man would pick up his tuning fork, tap it on the side of the wheelchair, and say, "That's middle C! It was middle C yesterday; it will be middle C tomorrow; it will be middle C a thousand years from now. The tenor upstairs sings flat. The piano across the hall is out of tune, but, my friend, that is middle C."

You and I need a middle C. Haven't you had enough change in your life? Relationships change. Health changes. The weather changes. But the Yahweh who ruled the earth last night is the same Yahweh who rules it today. Same convictions. Same plan. Same mood. Same love. He never changes. You can no more alter God than a pebble can alter the rhythm of the Pacific. Yahweh is our middle C. A still point in a turning world. Don't we need a still point? Don't we need an unchanging shepherd? (From *Traveling Light* by Max Lucado)

REACTION

6. How does Lucado's description of our unchanging God challenge you to keep changing and growing? What does it mean to "add to your faith"?

7. Why is self-discipline (self-control) so important?

8. What results from spiritual discipline?

9. How can a lack of discipline hinder your spiritual growth?

10. What is the difference between being disciplined and being legalistic?

11. What practical steps can you take to become more useful and productive as a Christian?

LIFE LESSONS

Spiritual disciplines are chosen pathways of spiritual growth. They are spiritual actions we take to train the soul. They are decisions we make to develop our spiritual sensitivity to God in certain areas. Since God is unchanging, "closeness" to him requires movement and change on *our* part, not his. In Jesus Christ, God has come toward us as far as he can. What are we doing to move in his direction? How are we deliberately becoming like Jesus? In what way will we imitate Christ today? Our answer will require some aspect of spiritual discipline.

DEVOTION

Father, you know our weaknesses. You know we are prone to be undisciplined in spiritual matters. We need you to come alongside us and help us. We ask you to guide us and give us perseverance and discipline so that we can grow in our knowledge of you. Let us not be content with less than your best. Show us how much more you want to teach us. May we always hear your voice and obey.

For more Bible passages on self-discipline (self-control), see Proverbs 1:1–7; 1 Thessalonians 5:6–8; 2 Timothy 1:7; Titus 1:7–8; 2:2–8; 1 Peter 1:13; 4:7.

To complete the books of 1 & 2 Peter during this twelve-part study, read 2 Peter 1:1–21.

JOURNALING

What spiritual discipline do I need to add to my life, and how should I start?

LESSON ELEVEN

FALSE
TEACHERS

MAX
LUCADO

REFLECTION

We are often impressed more with a teacher's style and charisma than with the veracity of his or her words. How do we avoid being taken in by an untruthful teacher? How can we avoid missing the benefits of a true instructor? Think of a time when you were impressed by a dynamic preacher. What do you remember most about the preacher's message?

SITUATION

Peter ended his first section with a brief description of Scripture and how God provided it for us. He begins this next section with a caution. God was the inspired source of the writing of his Word. Yet there were false prophets then and now. We ought not to be surprised that they still abound. As a safeguard, the old apostle provided a profile of false teachers and their fate.

OBSERVATION

Read 2 Peter 2:1–22 from the NCV or the NKJV.

NCV

¹There used to be false prophets among God's people, just as you will have some false teachers in your group. They will secretly teach things that are wrong—teachings that will cause people to be lost. They will even refuse to accept the Master, Jesus, who bought their freedom. So they will bring quick ruin on themselves. ²Many will follow their evil ways and say evil things about the way of truth. ³Those false teachers only want your money, so they will use you by telling you lies. Their judgment spoken against them long ago is still coming, and their ruin is certain.

⁴When angels sinned, God did not let them go free without punishment. He sent them to hell and put them in caves of darkness where they are being held for judgment. ⁵And God punished the world long ago when he brought a flood to the world that was full of people who were against him. But God saved Noah, who preached about being right with God, and seven other people with him. ⁶And God also destroyed the evil cities of Sodom and Gomorrah by burning them until they were ashes. He made those cities an example of what will happen to those who are against God. ⁷But he saved Lot from those cities. Lot, a good man, was troubled because of the filthy lives of evil people. ⁸(Lot was a good man, but because he lived with evil people every day, his good heart was hurt by the evil things he saw and heard.) ⁹So the Lord knows how to save those who serve him when troubles come. He will hold evil people and punish them, while waiting for the Judgment Day.

¹⁰That punishment is especially for those who live by doing the evil things their sinful selves want and who hate authority.

These false teachers are bold and do anything they want. They are not afraid to speak against the angels. ¹¹But even the angels, who are much stronger and more powerful than false teachers, do not accuse them with insults before the Lord. ¹²But these people speak against things they do not understand. They are like animals that act without thinking, animals born to be caught and killed. And, like animals, these false teachers will be destroyed. ¹³They have caused many people to suffer, so they themselves will suffer. That is their pay for what they have done. They take pleasure in openly doing evil, so they are like dirty spots and stains among you. They delight in trickery while eating meals with you. ¹⁴Every time they look at a woman they want her, and their desire for sin is never satisfied. They lead weak people into the trap of sin, and they have taught their hearts to be greedy. God will punish them! ¹⁵These false teachers left the right road and lost their way, following the way Balaam went. Balaam was the son of Beor, who loved being paid for doing wrong. ¹⁶But a donkey, which cannot talk, told Balaam he was sinning. It spoke with a man's voice and stopped the prophet's crazy thinking.

¹⁷Those false teachers are like springs without water and clouds blown by a storm. A place in the blackest darkness has been kept for them. ¹⁸They brag with words that mean nothing. By their evil desires they lead people into the trap of sin—people who are just beginning to escape from others who live in error. ¹⁹They promise them freedom, but they themselves are not free. They are slaves of things that will be destroyed. For people are slaves of anything that controls them. ²⁰They were made free from the evil in the world by knowing our Lord and Savior Jesus Christ. But if they return to evil things and those things control them, then it is worse for them than it was before. ²¹Yes, it would be better for them to have never known the right way than to know it and to turn away from the holy teaching that was given to them. ²²What they did is like this true saying: "A dog goes back to what it has thrown up," and, "After a pig is washed, it goes back and rolls in the mud."

NKJV

¹But there were also false prophets among the people, even as there will be false teachers among you, who will secretly bring in destructive heresies, even denying the Lord who

bought them, and bring on themselves swift destruction. ²And many will follow their destructive ways, because of whom the way of truth will be blasphemed. ³By covetousness they will exploit you with deceptive words; for a long time their judgment has not been idle, and their destruction does not slumber.

⁴For if God did not spare the angels who sinned, but cast them down to hell and delivered them into chains of darkness, to be reserved for judgment; ⁵and did not spare the ancient world, but saved Noah, one of eight people, a preacher of righteousness, bringing in the flood on the world of the ungodly; ⁶and turning the cities of Sodom and Gomorrah into ashes, condemned them to destruction, making them an example to those who afterward would live ungodly; ⁷and delivered righteous Lot, who was oppressed by the filthy conduct of the wicked

⁸(for that righteous man, dwelling among them, tormented his righteous soul from day to day by seeing and hearing their lawless deeds)—⁹then the Lord knows how to deliver the godly out of temptations and to reserve the unjust under punishment for the day of judgment, ¹⁰and especially those who walk according to the flesh in the lust of uncleanness and despise authority. They are presumptuous, self-willed. They are not afraid to speak evil of dignitaries, ¹¹whereas angels, who are greater in power and might, do not bring a reviling accusation against them before the Lord.

¹²But these, like natural brute beasts made to be caught and destroyed, speak evil of the things they do not understand, and will utterly perish in their own corruption, ¹³and will receive the wages of unrighteousness, as those who count it pleasure to carouse in the daytime. They are spots and blemishes, carousing in their own deceptions while they feast with you, ¹⁴having eyes full of adultery and that cannot cease from sin, enticing unstable souls. They have a heart trained in covetous practices, and are accursed children. ¹⁵They have forsaken the right way and gone astray, following the way of Balaam the son of Beor, who loved the wages of unrighteousness; ¹⁶but he was rebuked for his iniquity: a dumb donkey speaking with a man's voice restrained the madness of the prophet.

¹⁷These are wells without water, clouds carried by a tempest, for whom is reserved the blackness of darkness forever.

¹⁸For when they speak great swelling words of emptiness, they allure through the lusts of the flesh, through lewdness, the ones who have actually escaped from those who live in error. ¹⁹While they promise them liberty, they themselves are slaves of corruption; for by whom a person is overcome, by him also he is brought into bondage. ²⁰For if, after they have escaped the pollutions of the world through the knowledge of the Lord and Savior Jesus Christ, they are again entangled in them and overcome, the latter end is worse for them than the beginning. ²¹For it would have been better for them not to have known the way of righteousness, than having known it, to turn from the holy commandment delivered to them. ²²But it has happened to them according to the true proverb: "A dog returns to his own vomit," and, "a sow, having washed, to her wallowing in the mire."

EXPLORATION

1. Why do people follow false teachers?

2. What motivates false teachers to work their way into churches?

3. List several historical events that show God's justice.

4. What kind of tactics do false teachers use to gain followers?

5. Why will there be certain punishment for those who turn others away from God?

INSPIRATION

Two women: Miss America and Mother Teresa. One walks the boardwalk; the other works the alley. Two voices. One promises crowns, flowers, and crowds. The other promises service, surrender, and joy.

Now, I have nothing against beauty pageants (although I have my reservations about them). But I do have something against the lying voices that noise our world.

You've heard them. They tell you to swap your integrity for a new sale. To barter your convictions for an easy deal. To exchange your devotion for a quick thrill.

They whisper. They woo. They taunt. They tantalize. They flirt. They flatter. "Go ahead, it's OK." "Just wait until tomorrow." "Don't worry, no one will know." "How could anything that feels so right be so wrong?"

The voices of the crowd.

Our lives are Wall Streets of chaos, stock markets loud with demands. Grown men and women barking in a frenzied effort to get all they can before time runs out. "Buy. Sell. Trade. Swap. But whatever you do, do it fast—and loud."

A carnival of gray-flannel suits where no one smiles and everyone dashes.

An endless chorus of booming voices: some offering, some taking, and all screaming.

What do we do with the voices?

As I work on this manuscript, I'm seated at a desk in a hotel room. I'm away from home. Away from people who know me. Away from family members who love me.

Voices that encourage and affirm are distant.

But voices that tantalize and entice are near. Although the room is quiet, if I listen, their voices are crystal clear.

A placard on my nightstand invites me to a lounge in the lobby, where I can "make new friends in a relaxing atmosphere." An advertisement on top of the television promises me that with the request of a late-night adult movie my "fantasies will come true." In the phone book, several columns of escort services offer "love away from home . . ."

Voices. Some for pleasure. Some for power.

Some promise acceptance. Some promise tenderness. But all promise something.

Even the voices that Jesus heard promised something.

"After the people saw the miraculous sign that Jesus did, they began to say, 'Surely this is the Prophet who is to come into the world'" (John 6:14 NIV).

To the casual observer, these are the voices of victory. To the untrained ear, these are the sounds of triumph. What could be better? Five thousand men plus women and children proclaiming Christ to be the prophet. Thousands of voices swelling into a roar of revival, an ovation of adulation . . .

Jesus heard the voices. He heard the lurings. But he also heard someone else.

And when Jesus heard him, he sought him.

"Jesus, knowing that they intended to come and make him king by force, withdrew again to a mountain by himself" (John 6:15).

Jesus preferred to be alone with the true God rather than in a crowd with the wrong people.

Logic didn't tell him to dismiss the crowds. Conventional wisdom didn't tell him to turn his back on a willing army. No, it wasn't a voice from without that Jesus heard. It was a voice from within.

The mark of a sheep is its ability to hear the Shepherd's voice.

"The sheep listen to his voice. He calls his own sheep by name and leads them out" (John 10:3).

The mark of a disciple is his or her ability to hear the Master's voice. (From *In the Eye of the Storm* by Max Lucado)

REACTION

6. What makes false teachers popular today?

7. How can we recognize false teaching?

8. There are times when we need to confront and expose sin in the lives of other believers. What are some guidelines for deciding when this action is appropriate?

9. Why do we sometimes downplay God's justice and judgment?

10. How is it helpful to know that God has judged evil throughout history?

11. How can you guard against the influence of the sin in the lives of people around you?

LIFE LESSONS

Counterfeit money spotters spend a lot more time with the genuine articles than they spend with specific false versions. They are so familiar with the true bills that they almost instinctively sense something wrong with a counterfeit even before they identify the evidence of fraud. Our best defense against false teachers involves spending time with Jesus. The better we know him, the more likely it is we will spot someone bending or twisting his words. The more we listen to his voice, the sooner we will react to the falseness in someone else's voice, no matter how charming the individual may be.

DEVOTION

Heavenly Father, you are a just and fair God. You have promised to judge the wicked and reward the righteous, and we believe that you will keep your word. Please safeguard us from the influence of evil people. Help us to saturate ourselves with the truth of your Word, so that we will easily recognize and expose false teaching. Father, reveal to us your truth, so that we may walk in it.

For more Bible passages on the dangers of false teachers, see Isaiah 56:10–12; Jeremiah 23:2–4; 50:6; Ezekiel 34:2–10; Matthew 7:15–23; John 10:12–13; Philippians 1:15–17; 1 Timothy 6:3–5.

To complete the books of 1 & 2 Peter during this twelve-part study, read 2 Peter 2:1–22.

JOURNALING

What practical steps can I take to become a more discerning listener?

GOD IS IN
CONTROL

MAX
LUCADO

REFLECTION

Our prayer life represents a constant growing edge in our relationship with God. Prayers that ask get answered, though we don't get to determine *how* God will answer. Think of a time when you were disappointed in how God answered one of your prayers. What did it take for you to realize that God's answer was best for you?

SITUATION

In Peter's closing words he affirmed the hope we have as believers: Christ will return! And with him will come a fierce time of judgment. Peter added a strong endorsement of Paul's writings, affirming them as part of Scripture. He urged the believers to remember all the words of the prophets and the commands of Christ, and most of all, to remember that God is calling people to repentance and is in complete control.

OBSERVATION

Read 2 Peter 3:1–18 from the NCV or the NKJV.

NCV

¹My friends, this is the second letter I have written you to help your honest minds remember. ²I want you to think about the words the holy prophets spoke in the past, and remember the command our Lord and Savior gave us through your apostles. ³It is most important for you to understand what will happen in the last days. People will laugh at you. They will live doing the evil things they want to do. ⁴They will say, "Jesus promised to come again. Where is he? Our fathers have died, but the world continues the way it has been since it was made." ⁵But they do not want to remember what happened long ago. By the word of God heaven was made, and the earth was made from water and with water. ⁶Then the world was flooded and destroyed with water. ⁷And that same word of God is keeping heaven and earth that we now have in order to be destroyed by fire. They are being kept for the Judgment Day and the destruction of all who are against God.

[8]*But do not forget this one thing, dear friends: To the Lord one day is as a thousand years, and a thousand years is as one day.* [9]*The Lord is not slow in doing what he promised—the way some people understand slowness. But God is being patient with you. He does not want anyone to be lost, but he wants all people to change their hearts and lives.*

[10]*But the day of the Lord will come like a thief. The skies will disappear with a loud noise. Everything in them will be destroyed by fire, and the earth and everything in it will be burned up.*

[11]*In that way everything will be destroyed. So what kind of people should you be? You should live holy lives and serve God,* [12]*as you wait for and look forward to the coming of the day of God. When that day comes, the skies will be destroyed with fire, and everything in them will melt with heat.* [13]*But God made a promise to us, and we are waiting for a new heaven and a new earth where goodness lives.*

[14]*Dear friends, since you are waiting for this to happen, do your best to be without sin and without fault. Try to be at peace with God.* [15]*Remember that we are saved because our Lord is patient. Our dear brother Paul told you the same thing when he wrote to you with the wisdom that God gave him.* [16]*He writes about this in all his letters. Some things in Paul's letters are hard to understand, and people who are ignorant and weak in faith explain these things falsely. They also falsely explain the other Scriptures, but they are destroying themselves by doing this.*

[17]*Dear friends, since you already know about this, be careful. Do not let those evil people lead you away by the wrong they do. Be careful so you will not fall from your strong faith.* [18]*But grow in the grace and knowledge of our Lord and Savior Jesus Christ. Glory be to him now and forever! Amen.*

NKJV

[1]*Beloved, I now write to you this second epistle (in both of which I stir up your pure minds by way of reminder),* [2]*that you may be mindful of the words which were spoken before by the holy prophets, and of the commandment of us, the apostles of the Lord and Savior,* [3]*knowing this first: that scoffers will come in the last days, walking according to their own lusts,* [4]*and saying, "Where is the promise of His coming? For since the fathers fell asleep, all things continue as they were from the beginning of creation."* [5]*For this they willfully forget: that by the word of God the heavens were of old, and the earth standing out of water and in the water,* [6]*by which the world that then existed perished, being flooded with water.* [7]*But the heavens and the earth which are now preserved by the same word, are reserved for fire until the day of judgment and perdition of ungodly men.*

[8]*But, beloved, do not forget this one thing, that with the Lord one day is as a thousand years, and a thousand years as one day.* [9]*The Lord is not slack concerning His promise, as some count slackness, but is longsuffering toward us, not willing that any should perish but that all should come to repentance.*

[10]*But the day of the Lord will come as a thief in the night, in which the heavens will pass away with a great noise, and the elements will melt with fervent heat; both the*

earth and the works that are in it will be burned up. ¹¹Therefore, since all these things will be dissolved, what manner of persons ought you to be in holy conduct and godliness, ¹²looking for and hastening the coming of the day of God, because of which the heavens will be dissolved, being on fire, and the elements will melt with fervent heat? ¹³Nevertheless we, according to His promise, look for new heavens and a new earth in which righteousness dwells.

¹⁴Therefore, beloved, looking forward to these things, be diligent to be found by Him in peace, without spot and blameless; ¹⁵and consider that the longsuffering of our Lord is salvation—as also our beloved brother Paul, according to the wisdom given to him, has written to you, ¹⁶as also in all his epistles, speaking in them of these things, in which are some things hard to understand, which untaught and unstable people twist to their own destruction, as they do also the rest of the Scriptures.

¹⁷You therefore, beloved, since you know this beforehand, beware lest you also fall from your own steadfastness, being led away with the error of the wicked; ¹⁸but grow in the grace and knowledge of our Lord and Savior Jesus Christ.

To Him be the glory both now and forever. Amen.

EXPLORATION

1. Why is it important for us to know what to expect in the last days?

2. Explain why God is delaying his punishment of the wicked.

3. How can we be sure that God is in control?

4. In light of Christ's imminent return, describe how Peter tells us we should live our lives.

5. How can believers guard their faith?

INSPIRATION

Be honest. Are we glad he says no to what we want and yes to what we need? Not always. If we ask for a new marriage, and he says honor the one you've got, we aren't happy. If we ask for healing, and he says learn through the pain, we aren't happy. If we ask for more money, and he says treasure the unseen, we aren't always happy.

When God doesn't do what we want, it's not easy. Never has been. Never will be. But faith is the conviction that God knows more than we do about this life and he will get us through it.

Remember, disappointment is caused by unmet expectations. Disappointment is cured by revamped expectations.

I like that story about the fellow who went to the pet store in search of a singing parakeet. Seems he was a bachelor and his house was too quiet. The store owner had just the bird for him, so the man bought it. The next day the bachelor came home from work to a house full of music. He went to the cage to feed the bird and noticed for the first time that the parakeet had only one leg.

He felt cheated that he'd been sold a one-legged bird, so he called and complained.

"What do you want," the store owner responded, "a bird who can sing or a bird who can dance?" . . .

We need to hear that God is still in control. We need to hear that it's not over until he says so. We need to hear that life's mishaps and tragedies are not a reason to bail out. They are simply a reason to sit tight.

Corrie ten Boom used to say, "When the train goes through a tunnel and the world gets dark, do you jump out? Of course not. You sit still and trust the engineer to get you through." . . .

Next time you're disappointed, don't panic. Don't jump out. Don't give up. Just be patient and let God remind you he's still in control. It ain't over till it's over. (From *He Still Moves Stones* by Max Lucado)

REACTION

6. In what circumstances is it tempting to give up on God?

7. What are the dangers of unrealistic expectations?

8. How do the promises in this passage build up your faith and confidence in God?

9. Why do we sometimes turn away from God when we need him the most?

10. How can you remind yourself of the truth of this passage the next time you feel disappointed or discouraged?

11. What step of faith can you take to demonstrate your renewed trust in God?

LIFE LESSONS

Peter told his readers he intended to "stir up their minds" with his two letters. In what ways has he done that for you? Every other aspect of our life in Christ depends on the reliability of his Word and the assurance of his return. Waiting isn't easy. We may be tempted to accuse God of being "slack concerning his promise." But if we are learning to listen to his voice more and more clearly, we will hear what we need in his Word to keep us trusting. And we'll also find plenty to keep us busy while we're waiting for Christ's return!

DEVOTION

Father in heaven, forgive us for demanding that you answer our prayers as we want them to be answered. Help us to be patient and to remember that you are in control. Teach us to surrender our burdens to you and leave them at your feet. And Father, we thank you that you always do what is best for us.

For more Bible passages on trusting God, see Psalms 4:5; 20:7; 62:8; Proverbs 3:5; Isaiah 12:2; Nahum 1:7; Zephaniah 3:12; John 14:1–3; Acts 14:23; Hebrews 2:13.

To complete the books of 1 & 2 Peter during this twelve-part study, read 2 Peter 3:1–18.

JOURNALING

In what areas of my life have I doubted that God had my best interests at heart?

Lucado Life
Lesson Series

*Revised and updated, the Lucado Life Lessons series is perfect
for small group or individual use and includes intriguing questions
that will take you deeper into God's Word.*

THOMAS NELSON
Since 1798

Available at your local Christian Bookstore.